The Best of East Lothian's Wildlife

The top things to see ... and when!

Wood sorrel

First published in Great Britain in 2011 by
East Lothian Council
Countryside Section 2011

A catalogue record for this book is available from the British Library

ISBN 978-0-9569430-0-2

Printed by
Allander

Contents

Wood mouse

Foreword

This wee tome, light in touch and style, is intended to give you an insight into what are considered to be the best places in East Lothian to get close to nature. Our aim is to inspire, to get you out and about all through the year, marvelling at the great outdoors.

Each of the 10 chapters looks at a place in East Lothian and its special natural history interest.

In addition other features of particular interest to that site are indicated, together with directions of how to get there.

At the end of each chapter there is a challenge to find **four** species for that site. They are rated in order of difficulty, with a **one** star item being relatively easy to find, right up to a **five** star item where only luck and perseverance will ensure you are successful. But see how many you can find…

Good Luck!

Autumn evening view north east towards North Berwick from the Hopetoun monument

Introduction

- taking it all in from Hopetoun Monument

Distant Lammermuirs

Start your exploration of East Lothian's wildlife here!

Hopetoun has interests of its own, but it is the **views** in all directions (you can just about see everywhere mentioned in this guide) from the top of the hill, or, preferably the tower itself, that make this a spectacular place from which to begin your journey.

From the top you attain an excellent panorama of the **East Lothian landscape**. Rising to the South are the Lammermuir hills, covered in a patchwork of heather.

Adjacent to the open moorland is a mixture of woodland and upland stock farms. Here, marginal soil precluded arable farming for many years until the advent of fertilisers made more intensive working of the land such as this possible. But, prior to this, these grassy slopes were the home of sheep and cattle.

Looking up a big beech

Few cattle farms remain. Fewer still are the areas still given over to woodland, but it is the upland valleys where you may still explore some of the area's original woods. Other woods occur around the county, but are typically plantations of varying age and with trees species that are only sometime native to this part of the country.

Much of your view all around is now dominated by the large arable fields, indicative of the rich quality of the soil. These fields stretch right to the coastal strip, interspersed only by the odd geological lump, such as Traprain Law to your East, or North Berwick Law to the North East. Together they indicate a volcanic history and reflect the passage of the last ice age. These islands of igneous rocks are important areas of **semi-natural grassland** in a sea of manicured grain.

The Garleton hill ridge extends east from Hopetoun

As you cast your eye to the North, you can appreciate how important the **Firth of Forth** is in the context of the area's human and natural histories. Settlements litter the shore, but so does the wildlife – the **range** of sandy, muddy and rocky **habitats**, together with the sea itself, providing a variety of opportunities for plants and animals. Indeed the **focus** of this book is unashamedly coastal, blessed as the county is with wonderful areas to explore from Musselburgh down to Dunglass.

With that in mind, it is time to come down from the hill now and go looking for our first recommended site.

Hopetoun Monument

The tower was built in memory of **John, 4th Earl of Hopetoun**, an all-round big wig in the early c19, best known for capturing Napoleon and latterly becoming an MP. Well, you can't get it right always. The memorial plaque to him claims that this structure was built by *'a loyal and faithful tenantry'*; that loyalty was surely tested hauling up these huge blocks of sandstone of a dreich morning...

A trip up the tower **is not for the faint hearted**. You climb up 132 darkened spiral steps (a torch is useful), out onto an airy ledge, which, for many, is just a bit too airy. Don't worry if you cannot make it up, though, as the views from the tower's base alone are well worth the effort. Sadly, even getting to the foot of the tower requires a 15 minute hike up the hill, which is not recommended unless you are sure footed.

The tower looms above

HOW TO GET THERE

First Bus operate a service – No. 121 that passes by Hopetoun Monument and you can ask to be dropped off close by.

From Haddington, take the A6137 Haddington – Aberlady road. Near the top of the hill the B1343 turns off to the east. After 200m, as the road bends sharply, turn right and down into the car park.

Disabled access: Unfortunately not good.

A quite stunning male long-tailed duck in full winter regalia

01
Birds on the
Levenhall Links

Where better to start our wildlife tour than on the spoil heap of a power station? **Levenhall Links**, lying to the East side of Musselburgh, is just that. The nearby Cockenzie power station generated so much waste – known as fly ash, that somewhere was needed to put it. Levenhall was nearby, the mudflats on this side of the River Esk were enclosed by a sea wall and the land slowly created.

When to go?
Overall, best in winter for large wader numbers and wintering ducks. Spring / autumn for passage migrants.

The wader scrapes
About 1-2 hours either side of high water.

Sea watching
High water is when the birds come closest in.

From an ecological perspective, not ideal. Yet, from this unlikely beginning, the site has been landscaped to the extent that today its mixture of open water and grassland are favoured stopping over points for loads of birds. That **sea wall** is great too; it allows you at high water to get the closest views possible (but you'll still need a telescope or binoculars) of whatever is on the water. This is where we begin...

Fly

The wader scrapes without waders, but with Cockenzie power station

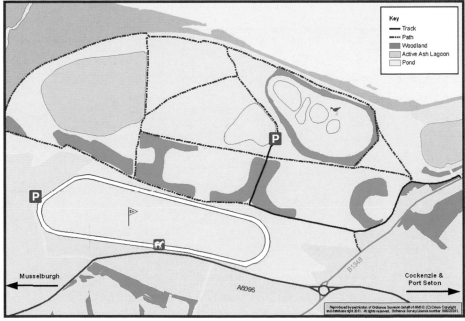

Key
— Track
--- Path
Woodland
Active Ash Lagoon
Pond

P

P

Musselburgh

A6095

B1348

Cockenzie &
Port Seton

Sea birds

Between **November – February** off the sea wall, you'll get perhaps the best views possible of a number of **sea ducks**. An identification book (see appendix), some binoculars and calm conditions really will open your eyes to a whole new world. Several species – **long-tailed duck**, **eider**, **common** and **velvet scoter**, **goldeneye**, **red-breasted merganser** and goosander – all patrol off-shore. Most are winter visitors from the Baltic area, seeking the relative calm of the inner Forth.

Right, punk duck! The spiky plumed male red breasted merganser. Females are grey with chestnut head colouring, easily confused with female goosanders which also occur here. Above, goldeneye pair, the male is turned towards you.

Left and above, male velvet scoter are identified by the white wing flash and eye liner. Females are all brown with 2 paler spots on their cheeks (but these can be hard to see).

Whilst the ducks all have compact rounded bodies with short necks, **other-shaped birds** are on the waves. Longer-necked and more streamline in profile, both **grebes** and **divers** frequent these waters at this time. **Great-crested grebes** are the largest of their family, then comes the red-necked. The two smallest grebes here are the black-necked and the Slavonian grebe. Any of these four can be present, so try to get an idea of relative size (again an identification book is invaluable).

You may confuse grebes with **cormorants** and **divers**. Both are bigger, though. Cormorants are all black with long necks, whilst divers in winter are feathered black and white, with shorter and thicker, necks. The **red-throated diver** is the most common here, and typically holds its bill pointing up slightly. Great northern and black-throated divers can occur, too.

Red-throated diver in winter and summer plumage – note 'pointing up' bill

Great-crested and a red-necked grebes. Difficult
to separate in poor light. The red-necked grebe's
yellow bill is a good feature, as its neck moults to
a pale grey in winter. Slavonian grebes are perhaps
the most common here, but easy to confuse with
their black-necked cousins.

FACT BOX 1 - BIRD IDENTIFICATION FOR THE TERRIFIED

There is, I am afraid, **no short-cut** to becoming an expert at identifying birds. But the **outright beginner** can have a go, armed with a guidebook, some binoculars, a notebook and a load of common sense. Here are some **handy hints** that will help you work out what you have seen.

Where am I?

You are in East Lothian, so **ignore** all those fancy birds from Europe in your book, they are unlikely to be here. Also are you looking at the sea, or in a conifer wood or on a farm track? Each of these habitats suit a particular group of birds

What time of year is it?

Birds **move around** – some come here for winter, others for summer. By getting to know these patterns again you can exclude many options

How big is that bird?

Birds are either small (robin), medium (mallard) or large (swan). There's much in between but get used to comparing one you know against another

Parts of a bird to look at

Often it is **little details** that count. Look at eye and leg colour, flashes of different colour on the wing and on the tail area, wing shape and so on. Note / sketch anything distinctive down, it will help

What about bird song?

Know a bird by sight? Now learn its **song**. But limit yourself to learning a couple each time only

How do I learn more?

Go out often in an area you can get to know (see chapter 10). Go also with an amenable bird watcher / bird group and you'll be given invaluable tips as to what to look for

Make mistakes

We all have, and we all learnt from them!

The bird reserve

Shallow pools have been created to provide the perfect place for birds to feed and roost, undisturbed by people. Many different **wading birds** (long legs and beaks, typically) come here at high water. **Bar-tailed godwit**, **curlew**, **redshank**, and **oystercatcher** and the tiny **dunlin** are the most common, but also (in season) look for **black-tailed godwit**, **knot**, **whimbrel** and **ruff**. Waders are amongst the trickiest to identify, so, if the chance arrives, ask a fellow watcher for some help.

Ducks favour these pools too, not sea ducks but **mallard**, **wigeon**, **teal** and other occasional visitors, such as the **shoveler** with its spoon-shaped bill.

Above. A lot of waders roosting...but can you identify them? (they are mostly bar-tailed godwits). Right, male shoveler

Ox-eye daisy

The grasslands

Semi-natural grasslands such as these are a precious wildlife commodity, with many having been given over to arable farming. Here, however, ground nesting birds such as **skylark**, nest in significant numbers. Mammals similarly occupy this niche, with **hares** and **foxes** playing out the eternal struggle of hunter and hunted.

Grasslands also enable **wild flowers** to flourish and animals that feed on them. Levenhall has healthy populations of **bird's foot trefoil**, **ox-eye daisy** and many other wild flowers that have become established here.

Hares, identified by their large ears with black tips and large yellow eyes

A skylark betrays its name by not singing in the air but from some hawthorn!

The boating pond

Winter is the best opportunity for seeing many **people's favourite** – the **kingfisher**. It tends to flit around the fringes, dropping down sharply to spear some fish. Otherwise swans and a few ducks make use of this habitat, along with canoeists, yachts and even the odd hardy swimmer!

Despite the colouring, kingfishers are shy and hard to see

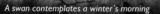

A swan contemplates a winter's morning

Elder pair

HOW TO GET THERE

Levenhall Links can be reached from the east side of the mouth of the River Esk in Musselburgh, and, from the west, along the John Muir Way from Prestonpans.

Lothian Buses numbers 26 & 44 pass by Levenhall Links. First Bus numbers 124 and 129 pass near by Levenhall.

From Edinburgh Waverley, Scotrail runs a regular service to the nearest station, Wallyford. From the station walk towards Musselburgh (along the A199) and then turn right at the roundabout (along the B1348), before finally turning left through a entrance gate (total distance, one km).

There is a car park adjacent to the boating pond which can be reached via an access road signposted from the B1348 coast road, approximately one km east of the Levenhall Roundabout.

Good. Access road takes you to the bird reserve and level paths provide access to the sea wall.

FOUND IT? WHEN SEEN -
Difficulty Rating (up to 5 stars)

Long-tailed duck		★★☆☆☆
Slavonian grebe		★★★★☆
Oystercatcher		★☆☆☆☆
Kingfisher		★★★★☆

02
Guddling in
North Berwick

Whether 5 or 55, the sheer joy of spending time **looking** for the beasties that live in **rock pools** is something that appeals to all. Although guddling can be carried out at a variety of places, **North Berwick** has pools up there with the best, together with offering refreshments a-plenty for when the work is done.

Guddling is best done an hour before **low tide** and on days when it's not too hot – better for you and the animals. If you **follow the advice** (Fact Box 2) you are certain to have a rewarding and safe time, together with ensuring that none of the animals you look at are harmed in any way.

Why North Berwick East beach is best

Whilst many of our shores are excellent places to delve for beasties, the **composition** of the shore on the east beach gives you a huge variety of pools, gullies and hollows to explore.

For the very young, the old paddling pond near the harbour end is an excellent, relatively sheltered area to introduce the world of the seashore and you are almost guaranteed to find hermit crabs, periwinkles and more.

Holdfasts, which are holding fast no more

the pools

North Berwick's East beach is the better beach to guddle

Seaweeds of the shore

You'll become acquainted with many **seaweeds** as you tiptoe over the rocks. In keeping with all plants, seaweeds need a mix of water, air and sunlight to grow. They also need to grip the ground – difficult when there's no soil about. So, rather than roots, seaweeds have features called **holdfasts**, which allow them to attach tightly onto rocks, in all but the worst weather.

Seaweeds come in **3 colours** – red, brown and greenish brown. Each **corresponds** roughly to whereabouts you are on the shore. Greeny-brown seaweeds (wracks) are found at the top of the shore, brown seaweeds (kelps) from the middle downwards, and red seaweeds further down still.

Rock pools, by interrupting the simplified slope of the shore, however, **contain more** a mix of seaweed types, which is another good reason to have a poke around them. See what you can find.

A mix of seaweeds from a rocky pool. The long strap-shaped kelp in the middle is called sugar kelp

Bladder wrack has pairs of air sacs on the stem

Spiral wrack twists and stem has a rib in the middle

Dulse, a delicate red seaweed of the lower shore

Channelled wrack, stem grooved on one side

Corallina, a brittle red seaweed that turns white when exposed to the air, often found washed up in this way

Knotted wrack has swollen sacs along the stems

Serrated wrack, toothed edges to stems

FACT BOX 2 - GUDDLE DAE'S AND DINNAE'S

Look after yourself

Rock pools are **slippery** places, so, don't go on your own, take your time when moving around. If you are out on a hot day, protect yourself from the sun too.

Be aware also of what the sea is doing. The **tides** go in and out twice each day – not so fast as you need to race – but check before you go by looking at the local tide times – see 'links' at the back. It's best to visit an hour or so before low water – giving you the most time and the largest area to look at.

Look after rock pool life

Animals and plants in rock pools need salt water to stay alive. So, if you are going to collect any for a longer look, you **must** have something to put them in temporarily. A shallow tray, filled with c. 5 cm of sea water is ideal – giving you a good view. Once you have finished, **carefully** pour everything back into a pool.

Most animals don't want to be caught and some should not be. A net helps for some creatures, for others use your hands. **Do not** pick up animals stuck onto rocks, e.g. limpet, sea anemone, and, if **picking up a crab**, grip the shell (carapace) carefully, but firmly at the top on each side above the claws as illustrated. Hold it elsewhere and you may get a nip!

If you **turn over any stones** to look for things, please carefully put the stone back exactly as you found it.

Rock Pool beasties

Not a great dinner guest...

There are loads. From fearsome **shore crabs**, to **hermit crabs**, **dog whelks** and **periwinkles**, by way of **worms** and **butterfish** and not forgetting **brittle stars** too. If you want to know what you found take a small identification guide with you or else, take photos and look at a website when you get home. (see recommendations for both in the appendix).

Did you know, that amongst the beasties you may find, the **bootlace worm** has the record of being the longest animal known? One washed up measuring 60m / 180ft.

Starfish have a nasty way of eating, they turn their stomachs inside out and force

it into their prey, which is then dissolved; slowly. **Dog whelks** aren't much better, they have an in-built drill that they use to bore into winkles to suck at the juicy snail's body. A tough world indeed.

Dog whelk (right), eyeing up its dinner – periwinkle (left)

HOW TO GET THERE

 First Bus link North Berwick to Edinburgh and the coastal villages in between and the 121 service connects North Berwick to Haddington.

Run every ½-1 hour from Edinburgh, dropping you on the west side of the town, from where it is a 15 minute stroll through the town and down to the beach.

Car users will find the centre of North Berwick busy with limited parking areas available.

Moderate. Car parks are located by the beach, but there are steps and slopes down to the sand itself.

FOUND IT? WHEN SEEN -

Difficulty Rating (up to 5 stars)

Bladder wrack		★★☆☆☆
Brittlestar		★★☆☆☆
Dog whelk		★☆☆☆☆
Bootlace worm		★★★★☆

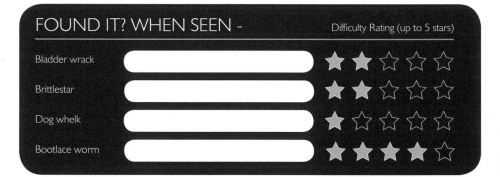

A hermit crab hides, a top shell sticks its head out and a rag worm passes by!

Beadlet anemone; remember animals stuck on rock should not be collected

Life in a rock pool

03
Coastal Colle

John Muir Country Park

Close by Dunbar, **John Muir Country Park** gives you a unique chance to experience **every** possible **feature** of the coast in one go. Cliffs? Yes. Sand dunes? Salt marsh? Estuary? Beach? Rocky shore? Even woodland? Yep, they're all here. This diversity of habitats means a diverse array of wildlife too and any exploration here will always be rewarding.

A view from the cliff top path on a stormy day

Where and when to go
Given the variety on offer here, any time is fine, it depends on what you are going for. Be aware that half the Park can disappear with each high tide, so plan your route accordingly.

ctive

Salt marsh and big sky, John Muir Country Park

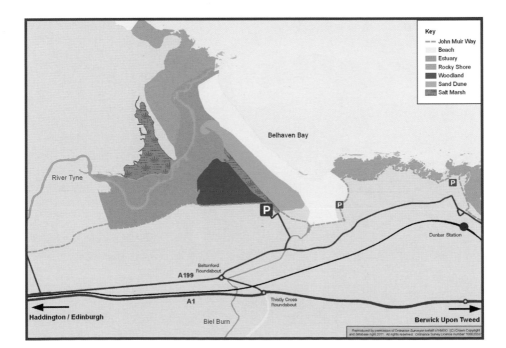

Key
- - - John Muir Way
Beach
Estuary
Rocky Shore
Woodland
Sand Dune
Salt Marsh

Belhaven Bay

River Tyne

P

P

P

Dunbar Station

Beltonford
Roundabout

A199

A1

Thistly Cross
Roundabout

Biel Burn

← Haddington / Edinburgh

Berwick Upon Tweed →

Don't call me a gull! Adult Kittiwake with chicks

Hard Rock

Between Belhaven Bay and Dunbar harbour, the coast rises to form an impressive sweep of **sandstone cliffs** and **volcanic exposures**, the path affording you great views of these and the view out to sea.

One of the best sights and sounds is the **kittiwake** colony at Dunbar Harbour. The birds congregate at the north end, where they nest on the ruins of the old castle. Each year, locals try to guess which day in February the first kittiwake will return. The colony is, with over 1,000 nests, the largest on a mainland man-made site in Scotland.

The birds have become used to human presence to a degree, so you can get excellent views. In full summer swing, the colony is extremely noisy and smelly, and don't wear your Sunday best as you are likely to get an aerial 'present' whilst you watch.

Kittiwakes can be **told apart** from other gulls by their smaller, gentler appearance and black legs. Best of all, though, they chant their own name – *'Kittiwaeeeeke.'*

FA▮ BOX 3 - WHO WAS JOHN MUIR?

To many, John Muir is a hero – the father of the **conservation movement.**

He spent his youth in Dunbar, gathering an enthusiasm for nature that would both stay with him and increase when his family emigrated to Wisconsin in 1849. Here, during some 40 years of wandering the US wilderness and through publishing a series of works, Muir advocated the **protection of areas of wild land**, influencing powerful figures along the way. Yosemite was the first location and subsequently, he and his followers went on to develop the **National Parks System** and the US conservation movement – the Sierra Club.

Indeed it is a little sad that today, Muir remains far better known over in the US as opposed to here. However, the **John Muir Way**, is an excellent long-distance footpath that winds from Musselburgh to the south of Dunbar, providing an excellent place from which to view the changing East Lothian landscape. **A book** of the walk route and features of interest along the way is widely available in local shops and at John Muir's Birthplace Museum. See appendix for details.

If you want to know more about Muir, a visit to the **John Muir Birthplace** – 126 High Street Dunbar – is essential. Again, details of how to get there are in the end section.

Soft Beds

Belhaven Bay provides a contrast to the cliffs of Dunbar. This expanse of **sandy beach**, backed by **dune and salt marsh** is popular with a variety of sports and recreational users all year round, but between the picnickers and the surf boards, there are some notable wildlife interests to seek out. Terns nest on the dunes and many other birds make this and the adjacent salt marsh their home.

Summer is the best time to look at some of the Park's **insect life**. **Butterflies** and day-flying moths are both colourful and plentiful if the weather is kind. Look for the distinctive caterpillars of the **cinnabar moth**, only ever found on ragwort, check around Linkfield car park. With more effort you'll also locate **burnet moths**. As for butterflies, **ringlets**, **small tortoiseshells**, **common blues** and **small heaths** are all about in June and July. The most scarce species, the **dark-green fritillary**, is found along the seaward edge of the pine plantation.

Belhaven beach, looking back to Dunbar

Not sure what you've found? Check the links at the back or compare to the pictures on the next page.

Small tortoiseshell

Small heath

Cinnabar moth caterpillar

Dark-green fritillary

Red admiral

Common blue

Ringlet

Burnet moth

Elf cups

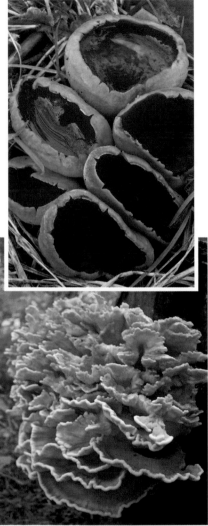

Chicken of the woods

*Sandwich tern, in
autumn plumage*

Into the woods

If the weather is against you, head in from the beach and salt marsh, to the pine plantation for some shelter. A damp **autumn** morning can be perked up by poking around looking for some of the **fungi** that occasionally pop up there. A couple of bright specimens found in the woods are scarlet elf cups and chicken of the woods.

Though few other fungi are so distinctive, it's always worth a delve to see what's around. But with over 4,000 species of fungi in the UK, you should admire these natural decomposers, rather than adding them to your bacon and eggs, as only the experts can tell which are edible and which will give you a nice visit to A & E. For advice on the best fungi field guide, see the appendix.

Muddy diners

The **Tyne estuary** serves as a **feeding station** for a variety of **birds**. In summer, **terns** – especially **sandwich terns**, patrol the shallows for small fish. The terns depart in late September for warmer climes; to be replaced by birds for whom the east coast of Scotland represents something of a warm winter break.

Whooper swans breed in Iceland, but their winters are taken in estuaries such as this, where they feed upon salt marsh plants.

Whoopers differ from our resident mute swan by having a yellow as opposed to orange, coloured bill. They can, however, be confused with another, very occasional visiting, winter swan – the Bewick's swan. Telling these two apart is a matter of some skill, the Bewick's swan being slightly smaller, stockier and with a more rounded head, less yellow at the base of the bill and thicker neck. But from a distance in the breeze, this can be very hard to determine.

Bewick's swan (left) and Whooper swan (right) embark on staring contest

HOW TO GET THERE

 First Bus services operate between Edinburgh and Dunbar, ask the driver to drop you off near the Park.

Scotrail services operate to Dunbar from both Edinburgh and from the south.

 Follow the A1. At the Thistly Cross Roundabout, take the turning towards Dunbar/East Linton/North Berwick. Arriving soon after at a second roundabout, turn right (along the A1087, signposted Dunbar). After one kilometre turn left and follow the signs into Linkfield car park which is clearly sign-posted.

Moderate. The car park at Shore Road gives a close view of Belhaven Bay. The kittiwake colony can be reached by parking in Dunbar Harbour.

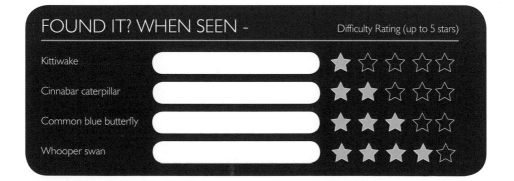

FOUND IT? WHEN SEEN -

Difficulty Rating (up to 5 stars)

		Difficulty Rating
Kittiwake		★ ☆ ☆ ☆ ☆
Cinnabar caterpillar		★ ★ ☆ ☆ ☆
Common blue butterfly		★ ★ ★ ☆ ☆
Whooper swan		★ ★ ★ ★ ☆

Left: little tern; middle: arctic tern; right: common tern

Distant lights of Edinburgh

04
Stravaiging the
Lammermuirs

There can surely be no more evocative (Lowland Scots) word than *'stravaig'*. It suggests a randomness to a walk, but liberation to one's roaming too. It perfectly encapsulates the pleasure to be taken from a ramble over the Lammermuirs. Until the wind turbines that is. Now, the vista is irretrievably impaired and the hills urbanised in a way that has, for many, changed their appeal for good.

And yet... if one selects a suitable route, and adopts a suitably sanguine attitude, this is still an incredible upland delight where one can *loup* a dyke, *shimmy* down a cleugh or envelope yourself in a *smirr o' rain*.

When to go

The Lammermuirs can be enjoyed right throughout the year, though if forced to choose, a walk in winter snow or a dawn stroll in May would be the best times to go; with a vote too for early autumn.

Gate across the route to Lammer Law

Lammermuirs

Looking west to Hopes reservoir and the shoulder of Lammer Law

The **passing seasons** are dramatically evidenced by changes across the moors.

A winter walk (or ski), presents the chance to spot one of the **mountain hares** that live here. White (winter) coats make for excellent camouflage, but you can usually get reasonable views, before they show you a clean pair of paws.

Mountain hares share their snowy quarters with little other obvious wildlife; but early in spring the hills awaken and echo to a rippling melody as **waders** return to **breed**. Amongst them, **curlew**, **lapwing**, **golden plover** and **dunlin** all vie for who has the flutiest voice. Go and find out for yourself which you prefer. All you'll need is somewhere to sit still and a way of identifying who is calling. There are lots of websites (see appendix) which can help you tell one bird call from another (just learn a few at a time).

Mountain hare needing a lesson in camouflage

Golden plover in breeding plumage

Above, Looking down to Traprain and North Berwick Laws from White Castle hill fort; Top right, A black darter dragonfly warms up on a rock; Right, Bumble bee on wild thyme

During summer, mountain hares swap their winter coat for a blue-grey version. Warmer days also produce a brief flowering of **upland** plants – a vital nectar source for a variety of insects.

Waterbodies are home to other insects. Some of these are hunters rather than herbivores. A local speciality is the black darter dragonfly, which, as a youngster lives in peaty pools, before emerging as an adult to bask on rocks close by.

Heather comes into flower near the end of August. It has long been managed for **red grouse**, whose rippling, gurgling call you'll most likely hear. The heather is allowed to grow until it becomes too tall for grouse to nest amongst, whereupon sections are burnt, in strips to promote new growth, during late winter, giving a patchwork appearance to the hills.

Managed heather moorland

Red grouse, males, such as this, have a thick red flash above the eye in summer

FACT BOX 4 - ACCESS TO THE HILLS

You can now, by law, **access** the hills freely, so long as you do so in a responsible manner. This means that you do so under your own steam (not an engine's) and that you **take heed** of what the wildlife and the people working on the hills are up to through the year.

Breeding birds and other animals

During spring / summer moorland birds are **nesting**. They do so on the **ground**; there's no choice. At these times it is essential you **do not disturb** them or their eggs, so (it is best to) stick to paths and do not linger if birds are agitated.

If you have a **dog** it must be either on a **short lead**, or under close control – i.e. a couple of metres from you and responsive to your command. Otherwise birds, lambs and cattle can all be disturbed and their young injured. You will be in a bit of bother, too.

Safety on the hills

The Lammermuirs can get enveloped in mist at any time and at others the **weather** can be just plain nasty. So, **go properly equipped**. Waterproofs, a map and compass and the ability to use them are the minimum skills and equipment you should have. Then think about spare clothes, food, drink, a first aid kit and letting someone know your planned route.

Do not rely on **mobile phones** as the **signal** is not consistent. Be aware that in early spring muirburn (burning heather) will be taking place and that August 12th is the start of the grouse **shooting season**. Shoots are organised and should be clearly indicated on the ground, but if you encounter a shoot, your access may be temporarily impaired.

Ticks and adders have both been encountered on the hills. Again, staying on defined paths is the best way of avoiding either of these.

A crisp midwinter's night is a great time to head up the hills for some stargazing. Once over the northern escarpment you are in a land with very little light pollution and the views are incredibly clear.

Chill midwinter full moon

A long-forgotten marker stone?

Whiteadder reservoir from Priestlaw

Place names of the Lammermuirs

The hills, cleughs (valleys) and burns of the Lammermuirs have a medley of names. Whilst some – *Windy Law, Snail's Cleugh* and *Sting Bank burn* – are a little unimaginative, others are much more **evocative**. Who was the monk of *Friardykes Dod?* Who was the lady referred to at *Elsie's Cleugh?* Yet other names hint **of lost wildlife** – when did the last howl utter from *Wolf's Cleugh?* Then there are the simply **mysterious**. How often did the banshees meet at *Witches Knowe?* Who was slain at *Slaughter Cleugh?* What sounds emanate from *Lute Law?* Discover these, the ancient forts and cairns that dot the summits and much more.

HOW TO GET THERE

If you and your bike are up to it, some of the moorland tracks are passable, allowing for all sorts of strenuous options. Check the link in the appendix for the 40 mile epic across from Longyester – Lauder and back.

Roads from both Gifford and Garvald will take you up onto the hills, from where a variety of tracks can be followed.

Not good. Limited access apart from roadside views.

FOUND IT? WHEN SEEN -

Difficulty Rating (up to 5 stars)

The view from Lammer Law		★★★★☆
Curlew calling		★★☆☆☆
Mountain hare		★★★☆☆
Black darter		★★★★☆

05

Looking up Longr

Longniddry

Nestled between the Forth and the coast road, **Longniddry Bents** is frequently overlooked, the masses heading instead to Gullane for that classic beach experience.

Even amongst those who do visit here, many remain inside their cars, admiring the view, or, at the other extreme, leap onto a windsurfer and ply across the safe waters provided by Longniddry's shallow bay.

In consequence, the **coastal grasslands** are rarely busy, and long may this remain the way, for this narrow strip is a **botanical delight.** So, swear yourself to secrecy, and read on...

When to go

This is a visit for summer. Late May through to early July will give you the widest choice of plants to admire. With 3 species in particular, responsible for proving colour to the grasslands. Longniddry Bents is made up of three car parks (1, 2 and 3!) and a stretch of ground adjacent to number 3 car park called Ferny Ness. Continuing east a narrow path allows you to extend your exploration to Gosford Bay.

Primrose

ddry's Bloomers

Cowslip

Cowslip gets its name from the Old English *cus lyppe* meaning "cow dung", as it believed to favour ground fertilized by cattle. Trust those romantic anglo-saxons!

It is a close **relative** of **primrose**, but bears clusters of drooping flowers from one stalk, whereas those of primrose occur individually on separate stalks, and do not droop. It is relatively early to flower, some years appearing in late April, though typically mid-May is when they peak.

Cowslip

Patch of bloody cranesbill

Bloody Cranesbill

Bloody Cranesbill is named after the **colour** of its petals and shape of its seed pods.

Its deep pink (20mm) flowers form colourful clumps in midsummer. The abundance of bloody cranesbill around Ferny Ness is unmatched anywhere else in East Lothian. The reason it is so dominant here is due to its ability to cope with the exposed location, together with a preference for calcium soils, which are in abundance. Beneath the soil lay several bands of seashells reflecting times when the **sea level** was much higher and shells collected here beneath the waves.

Close-up of seed head

A crane's bill for comparison!

Meadow cranesbill, is a close relation, with larger (30-40mm) bluer flowers

The **last** of our trio, is also the least common. Here, however, it thrives between Ferny Ness and Gosford Bay, again due to its preference for alkaline soils and as a result of judicious gardening by the local rabbits. By nibbling away the coarse grasses, rabbits have enabled the plant to spread in this locality. The densely packed, violet, bell-shaped flowers are out from late June onwards. Given its shape, you'd never guess what this plant is called... **clustered bellflower**. Honestly, all these unimaginative names; it's as if we were back in part of the Lammermuirs. How about **purple pixie's party hat**, at least?

In the pink...and white...and yellow. Besides these specific botanical delights, the grasslands have many other coastal flowers that you'll encounter during your search.

Thrift hugs the coastline. Narrow, leathery leaves help conserve fresh water in the plant in the face of the salty sea air. On rocky patches between it and the shore **silverweed** carves out a home for itself, its metallic leaves gleaming in the sun and conspicuous red stems trailing over the shore.

Top, clustered bellflowers; Middle, The young gardeners of Ferny Ness; Right, silverweed, whose leaves were believed to relieve sore feet if you stuffed them in your shoes

Thrift comes into flower as early as April

Bladder campion (right), named after the large, net-veined sacs behind the deeply cut white flowers, is one of a couple of species of the campion family to be found in the grasslands.

Common centaury (left) prefers drier, sandier soils, particularly at the east end of Ferny Ness. Its pink flowers, out from mid-June, grow in clusters and close up early in the afternoon.

Musk thistle (right), also found at Ferny Ness can be identified as it is the only thistle to have nodding flowers, as shown here.

Yellow flag iris (left) is a tall plant that favours the damp flushes between No.2 and No.3 car parks. The tall sword-shaped leaves can live up to their name if handled roughly, so, as is the advice for all wildlife, better to look rather than touch. In bloom from May.

FACT BOX 5 - COASTAL ETIQUETTE

No, this is not about what colour your swimsuit should be, but a reminder that the **coast is a draw** for people with **all manner of interests**. Kite-surfers, bird watchers, horse riders, anglers and dog walkers represent a fraction of hobbies and sports interests catered for along our coasts. Then there's the wildlife that somehow has to eke out a living in amongst all of this. So, simply put, assume always that when you go to the shore, someone or someone else may also be wanting to go there for an entirely different reason to your own. So, **enjoy** yourself, but **with respect** to others and pay particular heed not to **disturb** breeding animals and birds. Thank you!

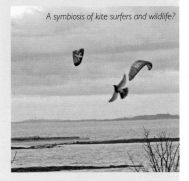
A symbiosis of kite surfers and wildlife?

HOW TO GET THERE

 First Bus services run past the eastern end of Longniddry Bents and will stop at the entrance to No.3 car park. Lothian Buses operate services between Edinburgh and Seton Sands holiday camp which is located adjacent to the west side of Longniddry Bents.

 Scotrail services stop at Longniddry railway station. From here it is a 15 minute stroll down to the coast

Three car parks off the B1348 / A198 provide good access to the facility.

Good. Car park no.3 gives good views of the coast and has a tarmac road around part of the site.

Gosford bay, next to Longniddry Bents, during the lowest tide of the year

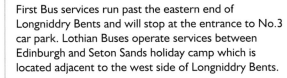

FOUND IT? WHEN SEEN -

Difficulty Rating (up to 5 stars)

		Difficulty Rating
Cowslip		★ ☆ ☆ ☆ ☆
Bloody Cranesbill		★ ☆ ☆ ☆ ☆
Clustered Bellflower		★ ★ ★ ☆ ☆
Musk Thistle		★ ★ ☆ ☆ ☆

06
Bass Instinct

Bass Rock

Not many **hermit refuges** or state **prisons** can claim to be a wildlife hotspot, but the Bass Rock is a little unusual perhaps. This volcanic plug, rising almost sheer out the Forth to a height of 106m / 316ft is the essence of impregnability and remoteness, hence its former appeal to monk and gaoler.

Before man ever made an impact, this **natural fortress** was, firstly, a perfect home for **seabirds**. Populations of different species have fluctuated over the centuries, but now, with a population breaching 120,000, the Bass is the single largest rock gannetry on the planet. David Attenborough described the trip around as "one of the top 12 wildlife experiences in the world". So, grab your waterproofs, camera, binoculars, and perhaps your *'kwells'* and sign up to a boat excursion you'll never forget.

When to go?
Being a trip made by boat, this is definitely not one for an inclement day. Indeed if the swell is too strong, the boats cannot go. So, be patient and try to get out when the weather is calm and in the period **between April and August**, when the colony is at its noisiest, busiest and smelliest!

Bass Rock in summer

Birds to see, hear and smell

Gannets completely dominate the Bass, making nests on any available space. Each pair mate for life and go through a ritual of honking / chuckling calls, combined with some bill fencing each time they are both at the nest. When one is ready to leave, it frequently points its bill to the sky as if saying 'right then, I'll be off, see you later'.

Adult gannets have crisp white bodies with black wing tips, together with a yellow head. It takes the birds 4 years to grow adult plumage, however, and you are likely to see younger birds with 'in-between' feathering.

FACT BOX 6 - GANNETS STATS AND FACTS

If there was an avian **top trumps,** you'd want to get the gannet in your hand. It'll either **win** or at worst come a close second...

- **Largest** British seabird – 1.8m wingspan

- **Chicks** at 4.5kg when fledging, easily outweigh their parents

- Built for speed and impact – **reinforced** head, throat pouch acts like an air bag, no external nostrils

- **Dive** for fish from up to 130 feet / 45 m above water hitting it at speeds in excess of 60 mph / 100kph; dives down to + 30 feet / 10m, stuns fish, swallows whole

- An estimated **152,000kg** of ammonia produced on the Bass each year by these guys

- ³/₄ of 1st yr birds don't survive. Those that do winter off west coast of Africa

- 4 years to reaching maturity. **Lifespan** typically 17 years, though some have reached 35 years+

- Adults can regularly travel **100+ miles** in search of food

Inaccessible ledges are the preferred nesting site of two similar looking members of the auk family – **razorbills** and **guillemots.**

Razorbills are black and white with a square ended bill, whereas guillemots are brown-black and white in colour with a pointed bill. Both species lay only one egg, the guillemot's being particularly pointed – supposedly to stop it rolling off into the sea.

Two other lookey-likey birds found on the Bass are **cormorants** and **shags.**

Of the two, cormorants are larger, with a heavier looking beak and in full breeding plumage have a white patch behind their yellow bill.

Above, razorbills; Top right, guillemots with young

The unique two headed cormorant!

Shag and young

A white patch can also sometimes be seen on their upper leg feathers during the breeding season. By contrast, shags in summer are all dark, and whose yellow bill colour does not extend around the eye. During breeding, adults also develop a distinctive plume, though this can be hard to see.

Other birds you are likely to see include kittiwakes and other gulls. **Fulmars**, a member of the petrel family, also nest in small colonies. These birds look like gulls wearing eye-liner, but in flight, their pale grey wings, held stiffly to allow for long glides, help you identify them.

You are **unlikely** to see **puffins** on the Bass. They nest in burrows, but there is little soil here. Instead they are on an adjacent island – Craigleith. Here, gentler, grassy slopes provide a perfect habitat. Repeat work by conservation teams is helping to rid the island of an invasive plant – tree mallow, which had threatened the colony by swamping the grassland. For details of how to volunteer your help, contact http://www.seabird.org/sospuffin.asp

Not a gull in Goth disguise but a fulmar. Get too close and you will get covered in 'fulmar oil', yuck!

Puffins at Craigleith swap fishing tactics

Bottlenose dolphins show off in style

Lastly, whilst concentrating on birds, don't forget to scan the water for other wildlife. **Common** and **grey seals** regularly bob around the Bass, and pods of **bottlenose dolphins** appear at irregular intervals, along with less common visitors including minke whale. Don't worry if you don't notice one of these, however, someone else on board will!

Common seal (left), note its snub nose, whereas the grey seal pup below shows their characteristic 'roman' nose

In winter the bleakness of the Bass comes to the fore

HOW TO GET THERE

Seabird Safari trips, organised by the Scottish Seabird Centre at http://www.seabird.org/ boat-trips.asp 01620 890202, visit via the RIB for a faster, bouncier affair. The seabird centre is also the only operator with landing rights onto the Bass, running specific trips for photographers.

Other operators at North Berwick and Dunbar can cater for private groups etc, and are advertised at the harbour.

FOUND IT? WHEN SEEN -

Difficulty Rating (up to 5 stars)

Animal	When Seen	Difficulty Rating
Gannet		★ ☆ ☆ ☆ ☆
Razorbill		★ ★ ☆ ☆ ☆
Grey Seal		★ ★ ☆ ☆ ☆
Bottlenose Dolphin		★ ★ ★ ★ ★

07

Rock bands & p

Barns Ness – Whitesands

Usefully, **rocks** don't move. Unless quarried or uplifted as a result of some seismic event, they hang around more a less for a long time. In so doing this means if you want to go somewhere to look at them, you can be pretty certain of achieving your goal. **Barns Ness** has rocks worth making that journey for. In fact, the rocks there get **geologists** very excited, (have you seen an excited geologist?) and you shall be excited too, by these and other specialities found along its shores.

When to go

The rocks can be enjoyed at any time of the year, but make sure **the tide is out**.

A rocky story

Walking from Whitesands to Barns Ness is to **step back** in time; between 360-290 million years, to be precise. This is because your route

Limestone hollows formed by ancient tree roots

ale lands

Whitesands shore and Barns Ness lighthouse

crosses several **rock exposures** which reflect the changes that occurred during these times. The features are explained fully in a **leaflet** produced by the Lothian and Borders Geoconservation group, available free at http://www.edinburghgeolsoc. org/downloads/rigsleaflet_barnsness.pdf. The leaflet guides you along the shore, **explaining the sequence** of sedimentary rocks that are there.

Sedimentary rocks, as the name implies, are made up of tiny bits of other stuff – old rocks, plant / animal matter and mud.

They form horizontal layers, lain down most commonly by water or wind, which over the millennia, become compacted, and possibly twisted and faulted by upheavals in the earth's crust.

An aerial view of the exposed beds

Multiple bands of sand, laid down when Scotland was part of a desert, compressed into sandstone

One type of sedimentary rock is **Limestone**. It comes in various forms, but tends to be white / pale in colour, as it is made up primarily of animal remains – bones and shells. Sometimes sedimentary rocks contain complete fossils; such is the case at Barns Ness. By identifying the fossilised animals, geologists were able to age the rocks themselves and work out the sequence in which they were produced.

Limestone was formerly quarried and burnt in the old kilns you pass here, to make quicklime, for use as a fertiliser and for the building industry. Today limestone is still being quarried, behind Barns Ness, where it is now used to make cement.

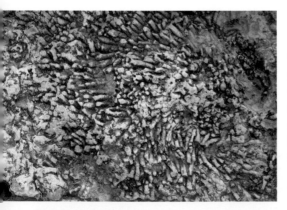

Spaghetti coral, or Siphodendron. This is a body fossil made up of a colonial coral, from a time when this area was a warm tropical sea

Fossils to be seen / Fossil collecting

There are many **fossils** to look for here, but also **rules** how to look for them. The **Scottish Fossil Code** (see appendix) contains detailed information about what you can and cannot do. Simply, do not dig out or hammer any of the rocks to look for fossils, instead limit yourself to looking amongst the exposed rocks of the shore. There's plenty enough to see there. Please take photographs, but leave the rocks for others to enjoy.

Pale carboniferous limestone, sits on fine beds of mudstone, which lie above a thin seam of coal.

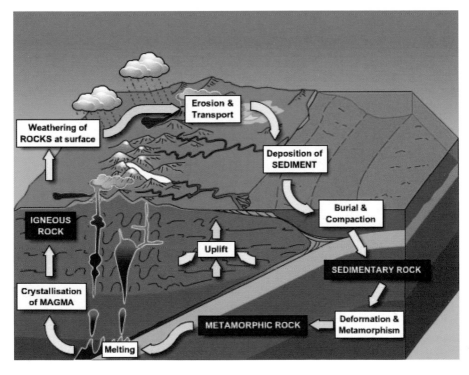

Rock cycle ©The Geological Society of London, www.geolsoc.org.uk

FACT BOX 7 - A BEGINNER'S GUIDE TO GEOLOGY

Geology = the study of rocks. **Rocks come in many types but belong to 3 groups;**

1. **IGNEOUS** – formed as a result of **volcanic activity**. Tend to be hard, (e.g. basalt) and as such are resistant to erosion and stay as upstanding features – e.g. North Berwick Law.

2. **SEDIMENTARY** – made up of horizontal layers, formed as sediments are gently lain down typically by water and air.

3. **METAMORPHIC** – either one of the above two groups, which as a result of enormous pressure and / or heat, has changed its form entirely. **Not many** of this type in East Lothian, except for the Lammermuir Hills.

Rocks get **worn down** by **weathering** – heat / cold / water and **erosion** – grinding away. They also get pushed up or dropped down hundreds of metres as a result of folding and faulting, when continents collided together. This affects their appearance.

Ice ages have shaped rocks even more, glaciers grinding away weaker rocks, leaving the harder ones even more visible (North Berwick Law again). The last ice age, ending about 10,000 years ago, will, of course, have left the most recent signs. Sea levels rose and fell with ice sheets leaving raised beaches.

Rocks are in a constant, long, **cycle** – they start off as a hard lump, get weathered (broken down), transported and eroded by water, ice, etc; before being deposited as tiny grains, often below sea level, and buried, where they may stay for millennia, compacting and hardening, until some force throws them off and up once again.

Birds of Barns Ness

Whilst a number of **birds** make Barns Ness their home, it is when these residents are joined by **'accidentals'** – birds off course – blown here by the weather or lost in the fog, or flocks of **passage migrants** that rest up here temporarily, that birders really start to salivate and which makes this place so special.

Fieldfare

Willow warbler pauses at Barns Ness

When to go – Though impossible to predict exactly, as a guide March-April and August – September, when there are north east or south east winds are usually the most productive, as these are the phases when migrants are moving through.

If you are fortunate, you may see flocks of exhausted birds that have hopped across the North Sea, such as **fieldfares**, together with one-off **rarities**, e.g. Pallas' warbler.

Tired and disorientated birds such as these tend to flop onto the nearest bit of cover to recuperate, so to find them, scan the bushes. Please do not disturb them by getting too close, however, as, being exhausted, the last thing you should do is finish off a bird by repeatedly forcing them to move.

Before leaving Barns Ness area, it is worth noting other features that make this a top countryside experience. First, several **coastal plants** abound, relatively undisturbed from trampling. **Sea wormwood** forms a distinctive clump in the hollow adjacent to the old lime kilns, with strongly aromatic flowers in bloom during August.

South of the lighthouse, the rabbit grazed grasslands are dotted with second late flowerer, **autumn gentian**.

These grasslands are also home to one of East Lothian's most elusive residents, **common lizards**. A tiny population hangs on in this area, and your only chance of seeing them is in April when they come out to bask in the early spring sunshine. Once summer comes along they are just too fast to see!

Autumn gentian on the grassland

Marram grass making patterns in the sand

HOW TO GET THERE

Located 4km south of Dunbar, the site can be reached by following the John Muir Way or easy cycle from the town.

Unfortunately, no buses go direct to Barns Ness – Whitesands, though No.253 Perrymans Buses can drop you off nearby.

The nearest train station is at Dunbar, some 4km to the north. Scotrail and Virgin cross country operate services to Dunbar.

Take the turning off the A1 onto the A1087 and then turn off again at the road signposted for both locations.

Moderate: Car parks near coast, but tracks are rough or sandy.

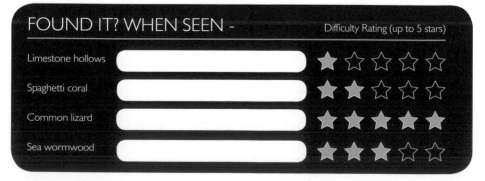

FOUND IT? WHEN SEEN -

Difficulty Rating (up to 5 stars)

		Rating
Limestone hollows		★ ☆ ☆ ☆ ☆
Spaghetti coral		★ ★ ☆ ☆ ☆
Common lizard		★ ★ ★ ★ ★
Sea wormwood		★ ★ ★ ☆ ☆

Common lizard heating up on my arm!

08

Where hobbits & elves ought dwell

Woodhall Dean

With so much fertile land given over to farming, **East Lothian** is one of the **least wooded** parts of the UK. Where woodlands exist, therefore, they are of importance locally to wildlife. Moreover, when these woods are of some age and relatively untouched by people, their (wildlife) interest increases yet further.

Woodhall Dean is a wonderful example of just such a wood. It is an **'ancient semi natural woodland'**. It has survived because it is located in a steep valley, which was of no value for agriculture.

A journey into the wood assaults the **senses**, from the twisting shapes of the trees, to the overpowering smell of some of its plants and the brief, but rich, harmony of its birdsong. So, enter within, become overwhelmed and get carried away in this land fit for a Tolkein fantasy.

When to go

A **spring visit** (late April-May) is recommended, being best for plants and birdsong. At the same time, the leaves on the trees will be fresh and young and still too small to cast a dense shade.

An excellent path will take you up the burn, out the woods and round back again. Allow 1 1/2 – 2 hours to complete.

Above, Wild garlic flower and bank

Next stop Mordor

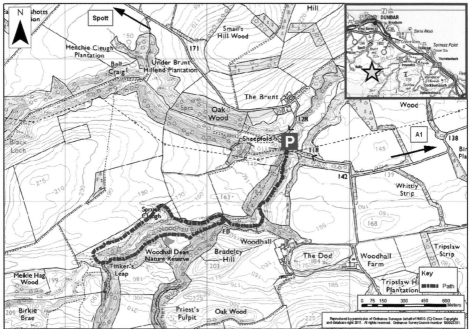

What you'll see

Woodhall Dean is a relic of the type of **deciduous woodland** that once would have covered much of the county. **Sessile oaks** have leaves with stems and acorns that do not (whereas the opposite is the case for pedunculate oaks). **Downy birch** trees make up much of the woodland, with a layer of **hazel** scrub forming patches beneath. On the ground many woodland plants abound, ground layer containing carpets of **wood rush**, **bluebell**, **wild garlic** and **wood sorrel**.

Rarer plants to look out for include **upland enchanter's nightshade**, **stone bramble**, and **wood vetch**. There are plenty ferns too in the damper areas, including two of local interest; **oak fern** and **brittle bladder fern**.

FACT BOX 8a - TELLING ONE TREE FROM THE OTHER

First of all, is your tree **broad-leaved** (deciduous) or **evergreen** (coniferous)? Telling the two apart is easy – in winter all the broad-leaved trees drop their leaves, whereas the evergreens retain theirs (except for one – larch).

Identifying individual broad-leaved trees is best done in **summer** when all the trees have their leaves, as they are the most useful feature to tell trees apart.

The **photographs** (not to scale) will help you get started with some common species. Most are **native**, but some (e.g. sycamore) have been introduced to this part of the country, albeit a long time ago and are referred to as **naturalised**.

There are only **3 native evergreen** trees – two of which, Scots pine and holly, you will find here. The third, juniper, is more of a shrub than tree and can only be found at the edges of the Lammermuirs. There are lots of non-native evergreen trees around, however, any walk into a forest plantation or formal garden will show you how difficult it can be to tell them apart.

Here be dragons...well not quite, but **adders** are frequent in Woodhall. In spring you are likely to come across them soaking up some sun on a suitable basking point – such as a rock, or even the main path itself. This should **not present** you with **a problem**, provided that if you have excited children or dogs with you, they are all kept under close control. Snakes have no interest in people and would rather slink off than become aggressive. So, if you find one, enjoy this unique chance to see a reptile close up, but for your and the snake's sakes, keep a respectful distance.

An adder warms up. Note the distinctive zigzag marking

Horse Chestnut

Ash

Birch

Alder

Rowan

Hazel

Scots pine

Elm

Sycamore

Oak

FACT BOX 8b - WOODN'T YOU LIKE TO KNOW?

When searching for wildlife in East Lothian woodlands, it helps to know what **type of wood** you are in. This can be assessed in various ways, but here are some guidelines to follow.

First, have a look at the trees around you in general. Are they all of one form – coniferous or deciduous, or a bit of both? Answering this will let you know whether you are in an **evergreen woodland**, a **broad leaved woodland** or a **mixed wood**.

Second, now look at the **structure** of the wood. Do all the trees look the same age (look at their height and girth)? Are they all in neat rows tightly packed together? If **yes**, you are in **plantation woodland**. These tend to be woods where growing timber is the priority. As such there's little room for wildlife, though some species will enjoy it.

If, however, your wood has **variety** in the age / size of **native** trees, this offers a greater potential for wildlife. A more **natural woodland** should have 3 obvious **layers** – a tree canopy, a shrub layer and last a ground layer of woodland plants that get just sufficient sunlight to be able to grow.

Ancient semi-natural woodlands, such as Woodhall Dean, have all of the features of a natural woodland, together with certain plants whose presence or absence is indicative of a wood's overall age, given these plants' preference for undisturbed woods. Three key plants are **wood anemone, dog's mercury** and **bluebell**. Find all of these and you are likely to be in an ancient semi-natural wood!

*Left, birch polypore
above, bluebell*

Top left, not native nor natural – a conifer plantation. Left, a planted broad leaved woodland at Yellowcraig. Above, better still, Butterdean wood shows a mix of ages and native woodland layers

Right, wood anemone; left, dog's mercury – both ancient woodland indicators

Birds of Woodhall

The work of **woodpeckers** is detectable on standing dead wood, where numerous holes reveal their drilling for beetle larvae. **Dippers** are frequently seen on the Woodhall Burn. Elsewhere **redstarts**, a rare breeder in East Lothian, nest amongst the oaks.

Woodpecker

Woodpecker was 'ere!

Male redstart

Many **mammals** are present here. You have a good chance of seeing evidence, at least, of **badgers**. Their bulky frames make distinctive tracks through the undergrowth. Did you know that unlike their English cousins, Scottish badgers do not hibernate – as being unable to lay up sufficient fat reserves each autumn, they have to get out whenever they can in winter, in order to top up their food.

Above right, dipper; they prefer fast flowing streams such as at Woodhall
Left, badger print – note the 5 pointed claws

HOW TO GET THERE

Getting to Woodhall Dean is a tricky endeavour. Sadly far from any bus route, even cyclists will do well to climb the tortuous lanes that lead to its entrance and many car drivers will simply get lost. Perhaps this is why it is so well preserved.

Take the road leading steeply South out of Spott village, or if coming from the A1, turn off at the Innerwick junction and after 1 mile turn right, and continue along for 2 miles before you cross a burn and reach the small lay-by adjacent to the entrance.

Bad. No access available.

FOUND IT? WHEN SEEN -
Difficulty Rating (up to 5 stars)

Wild garlic		★☆☆☆☆
Adder		★★★★☆
Dog's mercury		★★☆☆☆
Redstart		★★★★☆

09

The Dam Busters

Aberlady Bay

Every **October**, Aberlady Bay plays host to the aerial **spectacle of pink-footed geese** coming in to land on the Bay. At their peak, there can be up to 30,000 birds flying in at dusk, in V-shaped parties called 'skeins'.

Unlike a lot of other wildlife watching, the geese are easy to see, too. All you need to do is go to the small car park next to the Bay (well wrapped up) from anytime after 5pm, and wait. Soon, wave upon wave – think Dam Busters or Apocalypse Now – of geese will come in, normally from the east or south east, making their distinctive call as they approach.

Whilst most of the geese frequenting the Bay are of the pink-footed variety, keen eyes will be able to pick out at least 3 other species, together with a wide variety of ducks and waders that also inhabit the area.

The geese spectacle is at its best usually only for a few weeks from October to early November, as the birds come into roost on the safety of the mudflats.

Get down when the chance presents itself. A crisp, clear evening makes the experience all the more enjoyable too, you can even watch the geese flying in as the moon rises behind!

ABERLADY BAY LNR

# of Aberlady Bay

You can watch the geese from here

Altogether now; 'da-da-da-da-daaah dah!' Pink-footed geese

FACT BOX 9 - IDENTIFYING GEESE

Telling one goose from another requires the use of your **ears** as much as your **eyes** (but see the images on these pages).

There are **two grey geese** regularly seen in winter in East Lothian – the pink-footed, and the greylag. The greylag is bigger and makes the classic, honking, 'ang-ung-ung' sound – the same as domestic geese. To look at it has a large, pinky-orange bill, pinky-orange legs and a stocky grey body.

The pink-footed goose, unsurprisingly, has pink feet. Its head looks darker from a distance, contrasting with the grey body and its bill is darker too, with only a blob of pink colouring it. The most distinguishing feature is its call – a high pitch 'wik-wik'.

Now to **'black' geese**. First, the **barnacle goose** makes a brief appearance each Oct-Nov in East Lothian, en route to its wintering quarters of the Solway Firth. They have bold, contrasting, markings with a white blaze across the face, split by a black stripe from the bill to the eye. The rest of the head and neck is black, contrasting with paler blue-grey body and wing feathers. Their call is different – like a dog yapping.

You are only ever likely to confuse the barnacle with the **Canada goose**. These are larger though, and all have a white collar on the neck and a brown body. They don't normally turn up in winter, instead small parties come past in June and again in August – these being naturalised Canada geese from England which fly up to the Moray Firth each summer where they moult their feathers.

The third black goose you may come across is the **brent goose**. Much the smallest, they typically form parties of 5-15, and feed on the grasses on the mudflats. In colour the heads and necks are all black, with a faint white collar, the bodies brown, with either pale or dark bellies – depending upon which of the sub-species you encounter.

Two Barnacle geese, the one on the left is a youngster, growing in its adult feathers

Canada geese on the march, see how the white throat pattern and brown body differs from the Barnacles'

A pink-footed Greylag goose! Note orange bill, wait for the honk!

Below, Pink-footed geese, see how the head looks dark. By day they feed on the stubble fields around the county

A gaggle of geese, can you identify them and spot the rare Snow goose?!

Brent geese have only a hint of white on the neck

If you can identify these different geese, you'll be in a good position to pick out any rarer species that sometimes turn up amongst the big flocks.

To ensure you have spotted the right goose, always take a bird guide out with you, a notebook for writing down details or for doing a sketch and a set of binoculars. Back home you can always look at some of the excellent websites online that are there to help you identify birds. These are listed at the appendix.

More than just geese!

Aberlady Bay is host to a large variety of **other birds**, particularly during winter. If you look carefully you should be able to pick out a few different species of duck, for example, **shelduck** and **wigeon**; together with a number of **waders**. This latter group can be hard to separate as many species in winter all have varying degrees of grey plumage.

But you should be able to pick out the appropriately named redshank, together with a few more. A favourite is the **grey plover** – which is often seen singly around the Bay, though up to 400 can roost on the mudflats. In winter plumage, it is dappled light grey, with black legs and a 'soft' face – initially hard to identify. But when it flies, it reveals its unique identifying feature – black armpits!

Left and below, A grey plover showing off its distinctive feature

Redshanks feeding

Shelduck

Wigeon moulting feathers

Footbridge at dusk

HOW TO GET THERE

 A small car park is located ¹/₂ mile east of Aberlady village on the coast road.

First Bus 124 operate services that pass the Reserve car park. Ask to be dropped off there.

 Good. Park in the car park to watch the spectacle!

FOUND IT? WHEN SEEN -

Difficulty Rating (up to 5 stars)

Species		Rating
Pink-footed Goose		★★☆☆☆
Barnacle Goose		★★★★☆
Shelduck		★☆☆☆☆
Grey Plover		★★★☆☆

Emperor moth caterpillar

10

Aroondandabootabit

Your Local Patch

Having opened one's eyes to the wonders that exist around the county, it is fitting to **finish** with those **closer to home**. For, with due diligence, a host of fantastic wildlife experiences exist probably within a 10 minute walk of your front door.

It's making the time to look properly and the techniques to do it, that otherwise hinder us from realising this. But **take time**, enjoy getting to know your **local patch**, and you'll see there are numerous wildlife treats awaiting you that will equal any of those we have looked at so far.

Where to look and what to look for

Before you venture outside, consider some of your in-house guests. Some, like silverfish and wasps, are regarded as pests. Others, however, are positively beneficial to you. There'd be far more flies around if it weren't for the good deeds undertaken by the range of house **spiders** we play host to. The females are plumper than their male counterparts. Both can nip if threatened, so if you really don't like spiders and want them put outside, please go for the tried and tested technique of a glass and a piece of card which you slip neatly under them.

- your local patch

Hawthorn flowers

Hoverflies zoom in on a garden lunch

Pipistrelle bat rudely awakened

Some colonial wasps will not be a problem, as they make only small, and beautiful paper nests as shown here. Larger nests, however need expert handling.

Properties have gaps and cavities that mimic rocky ledges or old tree holes, which provide home for **bats** and **swifts**.

Both have lost a lot of their natural habitat and this is an example where a man-made structure has benefited wildlife. They are exceptionally good house guests too – clean, quiet, and with bats eating on average 10,000 midges each evening, what's not to be liked about them! Both are also **protected by law**, so if you do have any in your house, you cannot disturb them but must seek specialist advice.

Moving fractionally beyond the front door, check to see whether **swallows** or **house martins** have made their nests under your eaves. These birds winter in Africa, before making a perilous journey back to the area where they were born to raise their own young.

Right, Kids, they just don't know what's good for them...adult housemartin offers up a lacewing sandwich. Housemartins differ from swallows by having the white rump as seen here, and swallows have red throats

Above, male fern growing out from mortar on a wall; below moss doing the same

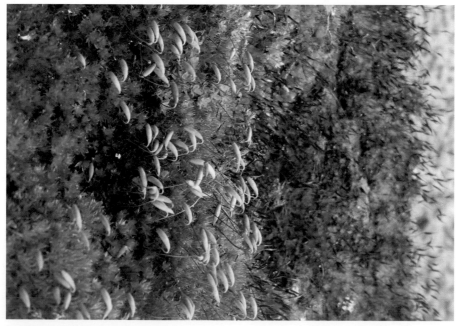

Once you are outside properly, check the walls – are there any plants attaching themselves to it? Have a good, close look. You'll be surprised how much may be going on.

For those with a garden, or even just a tree, the potential to get close up to some fantastic beasties is all the greater. The bark of a tree houses all sorts of goodies – animal and plant. As for a garden, a variety of native plants will attract a whole host of native insects and a few birds too. Look for **hoverflies** and **bees** sipping nectar, **red admiral butterflies** on buddleia bushes and **ladybirds** patrolling for a meal of aphids.

By night the cast of creatures changes – **moths** are attracted to garden plants and down on the ground many minibeasts are actively feeding. These creatures hide during daylight, but you can look for them then. Any old plant pot, log or compost heap should be inspected carefully and then replaced. Within these you'll find **woodlice**, **worms**, the **devil's coach horse beetle**, **millipedes** and **centipedes** to name but a few.

Above, Elephant hawk moth caterpillars are attracted to rosebay willowherb, a common urban fringe plant;
left, Pill woodlouse

Doorstepped by a wood mouse...a youngster extracts seeds from a doormat

More birds and mammals than you realise are attracted into gardens and areas close to where we live. Many, such as **blackbirds**, **great tits**, **hedgehogs** and **foxes** have learnt to take food left out for them.

Others are opportunists, feeding on something grown ornamentally. A great example is the arrival, most winters, of one of the most colourful of birds, the **waxwing**. When food runs out in their Scandinavian home, parties of these, starling-sized birds, make a daunting flight over the North Sea, arriving here half-starved. So, when they come across a suitable food source, they tend not to be too shy about getting stuck in. With care, you can

Best in show...waxwing eating hawthorn berries

get amazing views of these spectacular birds whilst they gorge themselves. Favoured foods are the **berries** of rowan trees and cotoneaster shrubs, both found widely in gardens and parks.

Most of us will live near fresh water of some sort. By getting to know a local feature like this regularly, you will be able to develop an excellent picture of what uses it and when. There's an annual pattern to the bird life on rivers and ponds, and a change in some of the species you see throughout the year too. Rivers in winter attract ducks including **goosander** and **goldeneye**, which depart each spring to breed elsewhere, leaving residents, such as the **dipper**, to nest in crevices along the banks.

Left, Male goosanders squabbling over the female
Above, Hedgehogs

Mink below (note white chin patch) and otter, above

Mammals too frequent fresh water. **Otters** are shy and wary but found across the county, though many people confuse them with the introduced **American mink**. Size separates them – an adult otter being comparable to a medium-sized dog, whereas mink are more akin to a cat.

FACT BOX 10 - FIELDCRAFT

There may be a **host** of birds, bugs and beasties at your doorstep and beyond, but this is of little use if you are not equipped in the **skills** to sneak up on them. **Consider** the following hints;

- Dress in **neutral clothing** – green / brown colours will help you blend in to most places, so wear clothes in these colours. Also avoid **fabrics** that **rustle**. If you want to get really close you should also **cover** any **exposed skin**.

- You **smell**. Nothing personal, but humans have a scent at the best of times. Add perfume and any self-respecting badger etc. will sniff you from miles away. So, leave off the smellies and try and have any wind coming towards you.

- **Get down**. Standing up and walking around, we tend to stick out, and can easily be an obvious **silhouette** against the background. Be prepared to crouch and crawl into the ideal position. Above all, **be patient**, wait once you are there.

- **Move slowly and quietly**. The first is easier than the second. I find walking on the outside edge of my boots and rolling the foot forwards makes less noise than thumping all my foot down in 'normal' walking fashion.

- **When to go**. Most animals and birds are active at dawn and dusk and get harder to see during the middle of the day. But it depends, butterflies and bats are two of the exceptions to this.

Smaller creatures are worth looking carefully for along watery edges and ponds. **Damselflies and dragonflies**, of which a few species reside here, can be seen on warm sunny days, patrolling over the water. They can be a little hard to identify at first. Begin by separating the two families from each other. Dragonflies tend to be larger, chunkier, with eyes that meet (or as near as possible meet) on the head, and who rest with their wings open. Damselflies are daintier, their eyes obviously separated, and who rest with their wings folded together.

To identify these colourful insects, refer to a guide in the appendix.

Above, dragonflies eyes meet like this
Below, azure-winged damselfly – note the folded wings

Spotted flycatcher

Left, nuthatch; below, comma butterfly, coming to you soon? Note its distinctive wavy edged wings

Go often

Repeat visits will allow you to pick up on changes – new arrivals or one-off visitors. With climate change and altering patterns of land-use, wild animals are responding to these alterations. Some are leaving us, for example there is a worrying decrease in the population of **spotted flycatchers**. In their place, however, **new species** are moving in. **Nuthatches** used to be unheard of in the county, but are now making inroads; along with the **comma butterfly**, which is fast being seen across East Lothian.

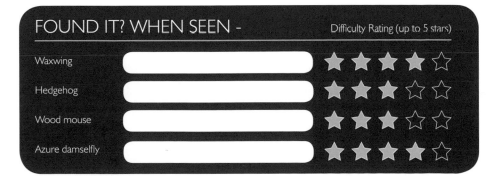

FOUND IT? WHEN SEEN -		Difficulty Rating (up to 5 stars)
Waxwing		★★★★☆
Hedgehog		★★★☆☆
Wood mouse		★★★☆☆
Azure damselfly		★★★★☆

Appendix

1. Recommended identification guides and other books;

Collins Bird Guide to Britain & Europe
Lars Svensson, ISBN 10-0007267266

Collins Gem Guide to the Seashore
Rosalind Fitter, ISBN 0-00-458824-X

Hamlyn Guide to Seashore and Shallow Seas of Britain & Europe
Andrew Campbell, ISBN 0-600-58376-7

The Pocket Guide to Butterflies of Great Britain & Ireland
Richard Lewington, ISBN10-0953139913

Field Guide to Dragonflies and damselflies of Britain & Ireland
Steve Brooks & Richard Lewington, ISBN13-9780954971311

Field Guide to the Bumblebees of Great Britain and Ireland
Mike Edwards, ISBN 0-953-11994-8

Mushrooms
Roger Phillips, ISBN 0-330-26441-9

The Wild Flowers of Britain and Ireland: A New Guide to Our Wild Flowers
Marjorie Blamey, Richard Fitter, and Alastair Fitter, ISBN 0-7136-5944-0

Walking the John Muir Way
Robert Russell, ISBN 978-0-9555851-4-2

Concise Guide to Moths of Great Britain and Ireland
Martin Townsend and Paul Waring,
ISBN 0-953-13996-5

2. Recommended identification websites:

Birds http://www.rspb.org.uk/wildlife/birdguide/name

Butterflies http://www.ukbutterflies.co.uk

Dragonflies & damselflies http://www.dragonflysoc.org.uk/species.html

Ladybirds http://www.ladybird-survey.org/downloads/Ladybird%20descriptions_Info%20pack_2006_v.1.3.pdf

Trees http://www-saps.plantsci.cam.ac.uk/trees/index.htm

Flowers http://www.botanicalkeys.co.uk/flora/

If you do not know what you have found, you can send it here and other people will try to identify it for you

http://www.ispot.org.uk/

East Lothian geology, including the Barns Ness leaflet, is covered by

http://www.edinburghgeolsoc.org/r_download.html
Scottish fossil code; http://www.snh.gov.uk/docs/B572665.pdf

3. Travel Information

General enquiries: Travelline 0871 200 22 33
http://www.travelinescotland.com/welcome.do

Trains: Scotrail and Virgin cross country
http://www.scotrail.co.uk
http://www.crosscountrytrains.co.uk

Buses: Lothian Buses - http://www.lothianbuses.com
First Bus - http://www.firstgroup.com/ukbus/scotland_east
Perrymans Buses - http://www.perrymansbuses.co.uk
Eve coaches - http://www.eveinfo.co.uk

Cycling: In the Lammermuirs
http://www.bikeroutes.org.uk/routes/watchwat.htm

Some cycle routes around East Lothian
http://www.cycle-route.com/routes/Round_East_Lothian-
Cycle-Route-152.html

Photography credits

East Lothian Council

Lorne Gill @ Scottish Natural Heritage

Steve Round

Elisa Smith

Jim Wood

Abbie Marland

Robin Redfern

4. Some useful contacts

East Lothian Countryside Ranger Service

The aim of the East Lothian Countryside Ranger Service is to provide an awareness and understanding of the countryside; enhance the variety of people's experiences provided by East Lothian's countryside and coastal sites and to ensure these sites are managed in a sustainable manner.

For all enquiries please contact ranger@eastlothian.gov.uk or tel. 01620 827279

John Muir Birthplace Trust all details are at; http://www.jmbt.org.uk

Tide tables

The tide tables linked here are for Dunbar, tide times vary a little around the coast of East Lothian, so, if you want to be exact, navigate to a suitable port.

This lets you know tides for the following 7 days.

http://www.bbc.co.uk/weather/coast/tides/tides.shtml?date=20110112&loc=0222

Coastguard

Can be contacted for general enquiries (e.g. tide times) on 01333 450666. In an emergency situation, dial 999 and ask for 'coastguard'

SSPCA

If you come across any injured animal, please report it to the Scottish Society for the Prevention of Cruelty to Animals at;http://www.scottishspca.org

Scottish Outdoor Access Code (SOAC)

A full explanation of your rights and responsibilities when accessing the countryside can be found at www.outdooraccess-scotland.com

Know the Code before you go... Enjoy Scotland's outdoors - responsibly!

Everyone has the right to be on most land and inland water providing they act responsibly. Your access rights and responsibilities are explained fully in the Scottish Outdoor Access Code.

Whether you're in the outdoors or managing the outdoors, the key things are to:

- take responsibility for your own actions
- respect the interests of other people
- care for the environment

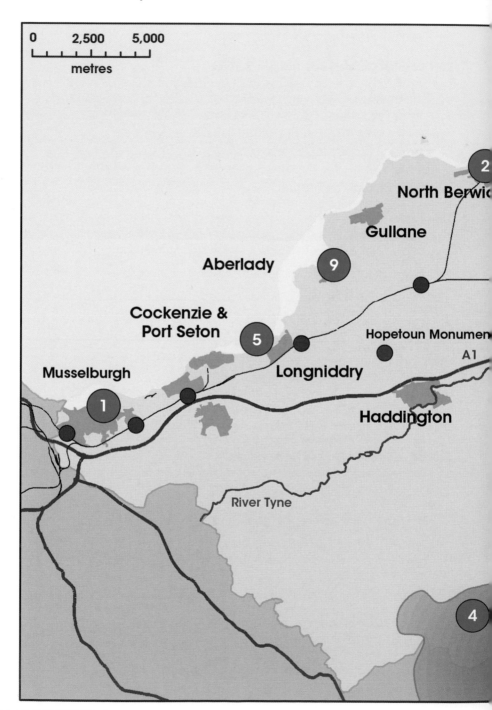

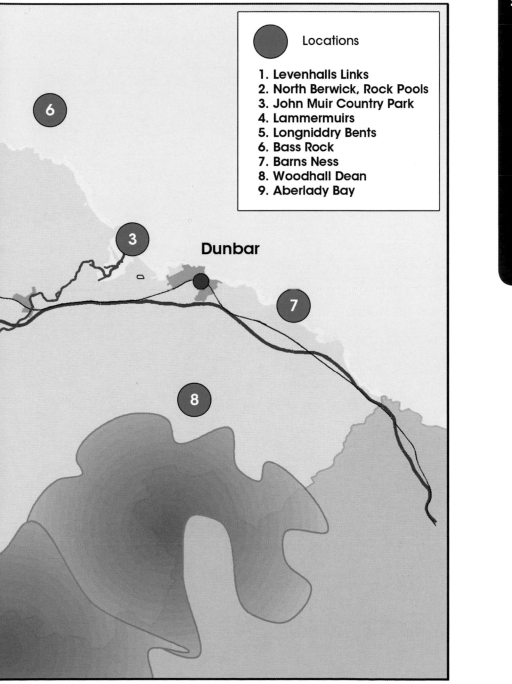

Locations

1. Levenhalls Links
2. North Berwick, Rock Pools
3. John Muir Country Park
4. Lammermuirs
5. Longniddry Bents
6. Bass Rock
7. Barns Ness
8. Woodhall Dean
9. Aberlady Bay

Dunbar

MAP | 91